EVERYTHING YOU NEED TO

MASTER

MINECRAFT EARTH

KINGFISHER
LONDON & NEW YORK

Copyright © Macmillan Publishers International Ltd 2020
Published in the United States by Kingfisher
120 Broadway, New York, NY 10271
Kingfisher is an imprint of Macmillan Children's Books, London
All rights reserved.

Distributed in the U.S. and Canada by Macmillan,
120 Broadway, New York, NY 10271

This book is not endorsed by Mojang Synergies AB. Minecraft and
Minecraft character names are trademarks of Mojang Synergies AB.
All screenshots and images of Minecraft and Minecraft Earth characters/gameplay © Mojang Synergies AB.
Contents based on Minecraft Earth early access. All information correct as of February 2020.

Library of Congress Cataloging-in-Publication data has been applied for.

Written by Ed Jefferson
Designed, edited and project managed by Dynamo Limited

Kingfisher books are available for special promotions and premiums.
For details contact: Special Markets Department, Macmillan,
120 Broadway, New York, NY 10271.

For more information, please visit
www.kingfisherbooks.com

EVERYTHING YOU NEED TO
MASTER
MINECRAFT EARTH

KINGFISHER
LONDON & NEW YORK

BY ED JEFFERSON

CONTENTS

WELCOME!

FOR OVER TEN YEARS, MINECRAFT HAS BEEN LETTING PLAYERS EXPLORE, BUILD, AND BATTLE IN VIRTUAL WORLDS. NOW THE NEW MOBILE GAME MINECRAFT EARTH IS USING AUGMENTED REALITY TECHNOLOGY TO TAKE THOSE EXPERIENCES INTO THE REAL WORLD . . .

If you're embarking on this new gaming adventure, this guide offers all the tips and tricks you need to get the most out of the game, whether you're out and about looking for action or planning your next build at home.

Minecraft's on tour—find adventures all over your local area!

Mobs as you've never seen them before—in your own living room!

GETTING STARTED

FIRST THINGS FIRST: YOU'LL NEED TO GET THE GAME RUNNING ON YOUR DEVICE. HEAD TO THE APP STORE (IF USING AN IPHONE) OR THE PLAY STORE (IF USING ANDROID), SEARCH FOR "MINECRAFT EARTH" AND GET IT INSTALLED.

The first time you run the app, it will download some extra content, so you'll want to be connected to WiFi. It will then ask you to create or sign into a Microsoft account—you'll only need to do this once.

Once you've logged in, you can either customize your character (see pages 8–9) or go straight into the game, which will lead you through a brief tutorial.

You can have multiple accounts registered on the same device—to switch to another account, you just need to sign out (see page 45).

Check the weather forecast before you play. Much of the game involves using your device for extended periods outside, so if it's raining you might want to bring an umbrella.

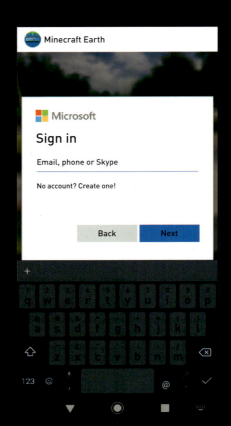

The Microsoft account screen

The game isn't designed to be played in a moving vehicle—you won't be able to collect items if the game detects that you're moving fast.

The AR (augmented reality) parts of the game won't function in dark environments, so the parts of the game that require being outdoors might not function at night.

TOO FAST!

Never play this game while driving. Safety first!

I'M NOT DRIVING

Uh oh! It's too dark in here! Move to a more brightly lit area.

At certain points, the game will prompt you for access to:

+ Your location
+ Your device's camera

You need to grant both permissions for the full Minecraft Earth experience.

Even if you're familiar with the original Minecraft, there are few things to bear in mind before starting on your new Minecraft Earth adventure.

BEWARE!

It's easy to get caught up in the game, but remember, you are still in the real world, too—always be aware of your surroundings.

CHARACTER CREATION

WHETHER YOU'RE PLANNING ON PLAYING ALONE OR TEAMING UP WITH OTHERS, WHY NOT GIVE YOUR CHARACTER A DISTINCTIVE LOOK? YOU CAN CREATE AND STORE UP TO FIVE DIFFERENT CHARACTERS OR LOOKS ON YOUR PROFILE.

Some items cost Minecoins, which have to be purchased using real money. Check with whoever pays the bill for purchases on the device before doing this.

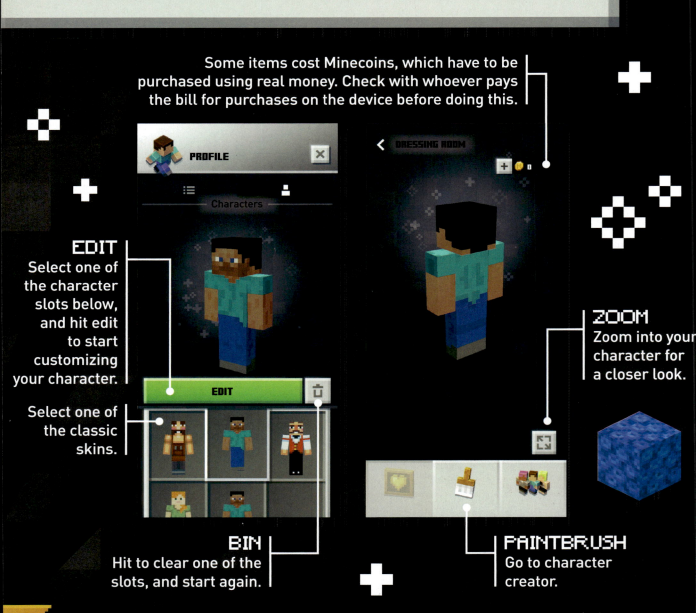

EDIT
Select one of the character slots below, and hit edit to start customizing your character.

Select one of the classic skins.

ZOOM
Zoom into your character for a closer look.

BIN
Hit to clear one of the slots, and start again.

PAINTBRUSH
Go to character creator.

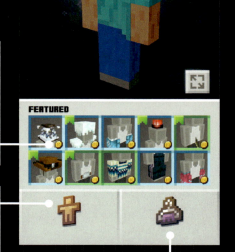

FEATURED

Once you have selected an icon at the bottom of the screen, select your chosen clothing or body part—with some items you can also customize the color.

The Minecoin symbol indicates that you need to purchase the item before use.

Adjust your character's body, skin, and hair.

Select clothes and outfits in the dressing room.

Select an icon to choose the type of clothing or body part you wish to change.

BEWARE!

You don't have to spend real money to get the most out of Minecraft Earth. In fact, you might get more of a sense of achievement by mastering the game without spending a penny!

Now, on to the game . . .

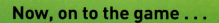

THE MAP SCREEN IS THE HEART OF MINECRAFT EARTH, SO YOU'LL NEED TO UNDERSTAND IT TO NAVIGATE THE GAME—AND THE REAL WORLD!

Although the game's map may not look much like the real world at first glance, it is based on it. As you move around with your device, you'll see your character walking around the map.

PUBLIC FOOTPATHS

BUILDINGS AND OTHER STRUCTURES

ROADS
Always be aware of traffic!

OTHER ACCESSIBLE SIDEWALKS AND FOOTPATHS

BEWARE!

The Minecraft Earth map is based on real maps, but always pay attention to what's around you and never rely entirely on it. A path shown on the map may have become overgrown or blocked, or it may pass through a park that is closed at certain times of day.

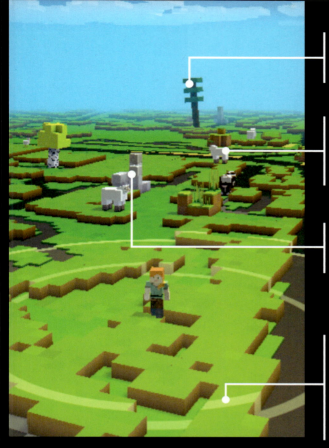

TREE
Tap these to gain some ever-handy wood blocks.

ANIMAL
Tap animal mobs such as sheep and chickens to collect them for later use.

GRAY/GREEN BLOCK
These block piles will provide you with basic building materials.

PLAY CIRCLE
You can interact with any object within this circle—walk in the direction of what you want, and it'll get a slight glow once you're close enough.

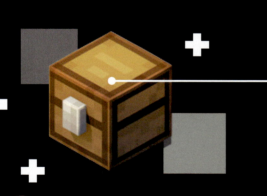

CHEST
Open for a surprise— it could be anything from wool to some TNT!

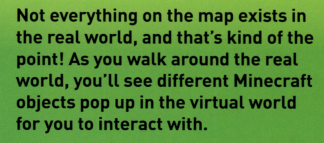

Not everything on the map exists in the real world, and that's kind of the point! As you walk around the real world, you'll see different Minecraft objects pop up in the virtual world for you to interact with.

PROFILE ESSENTIALS

YOUR PROFILE ALLOWS YOU TO KEEP TRACK OF YOUR PROGRESS IN THE GAME, AS WELL AS ACCESS THE CHARACTER CREATOR.

To access your profile, tap the head icon in the top left corner of the map screen.

Tap your character to access the character creator (see pages 8–9).

This is your current level and your progress toward the next. It is also shown on the map screen.

level **11** 2,824/4,300

Total blocks placed — 319   2612   151   2h 23m — Time spent in adventures or buildplates

Total blocks collected

Total mobs collected

PROFILE

Overview

minecrafter 1485

Your inventory screen shows the blocks and items you currently hold, and it allows you to select which items you'll take into adventures. Access the inventory by tapping the box item on the map screen.

INVENTORY

Select a category to see only blocks or items of that type.

SEARCH
Search for a block or item by name.

SORT
Sort items by name, quantity, or rarity.

All items

ITEMS
The number indicates how many of each you have in your inventory. The color indicates its rarity (see pages 24–25).

984   662   312   279
123   122   107   107
103   101   76   74
70   61   58   56
51   46   42   40

HOTBAR
Move items that you want to use in adventures or buildplates to the hotbar. You can't change these items once you've started an adventure, so choose carefully.

62   16   64   64   88

To switch to a different profile/account, you need to access the settings menu and select sign out (see page 45).

BUILDPLATE BASICS

THIS WOULDN'T BE MINECRAFT WITHOUT THE ABILITY TO MAKE THINGS. TAP THE BUILDPLATE ICON ON THE MAP SCREEN TO ACCESS THEM, AND GET BUILDING!

BUILDPLATES

MORE IN THE STORE!

just now

8×8

BUILD

You can purchase extra buildplates in the store using rubies. Collect them during the game, or make in-game purchases.

Here you can see when you last accessed this buildplate and the size (from 8 x 8 to 32 x 32 blocks).

Build mode will let you project a small version of the plate at home to let you focus on getting your build just right. Once you've entered build mode, you can start making adjustments.

Enter play mode (see page 16).

just now

8×8

You'll unlock a new buildplate for every five levels you gain during the game.

PLACE

While in interact mode, swipe underneath your build to rotate back and forth, so you can access it from a different angle.

INTERACT MODE
You can throw switches or open doors.

PICKUP MODE
Blocks and items you tap on will be picked up.

You might find it convenient to place your buildplate on a desk or table, so that you can sit down while working on it. Textured surfaces work better than plain surfaces to build on.

CUSTOMIZE YOUR BUILDPLATES AT HOME. ONCE THEY'RE PERFECT, TAKE THEM OUTSIDE TO SEE THEM AT GLORIOUS FULL SCALE IN PLAY MODE.

Access the menu to change settings or exit the buildplate.

MOBS

You can drop mobs into your buildplates—but be warned, hostile mobs will attack when you access the build in play mode!

You can expand your builds up or even downward, though you can't dig or build outside of the buildplate's width.

INVENTORY

Access your full inventory, where you can swap different items into your hotbar.

Select a block here, and then tap on your build to place it. Select an item and you can use it on your build

In play mode, your build is projected at a much bigger size, so you may find you need to head outside or into a larger room

Keep an eye on your health, as in play mode you can take damage from hostile mobs.

Any changes you make in play mode will revert once you leave.

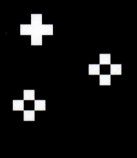

Any blocks you pick up will disappear from your inventory when you leave.

You can't access your full inventory in play mode, so make sure you've moved any items you want to use to the hotbar.

BUILDPLATES: CONSTRUCTION TIPS

Many blocks will float if you remove the block beneath them, so you can place objects in midair. Don't try this with gravel and sand blocks, though—they will fall to fill the space.

Torches, levers, and buttons can be placed on the side or on top of solid blocks.

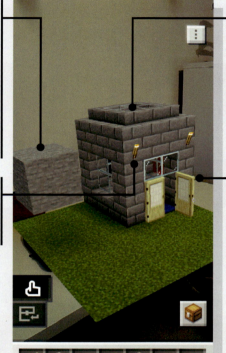

You can add more detail to builds using the step versions of blocks—the direction the block will be placed in depends on the direction you're facing, so you may need to rotate the plate or move your device to get the desired effect.

Doors open or close when you interact with them. They must be placed on top of blocks, and their position depends on where you are standing in relation to the block you place them on.

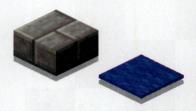

ROOKIE ERROR!
This door is on the same block as in the previous picture but placed from the other direction, so it is out of line with the door frame.

If blocks of glass seem a little thick for the window you had in mind, you can craft six glass blocks into sixteen panes of glass.

You can place squares of carpet on top of blocks, but you can't then place anything on top of the carpet. And remember, you can't have a door open inward onto a carpeted block.

If you're having trouble seeing into the interior of a structure, you can move your device through the walls to find a better angle.

BUILDPLATES: FARMING AND MOBS

SQUARE OF FARMLAND
To prepare farmland, use a hoe on a block of dirt.

WATER
Place a water source near your farmland to hydrate it, and your crops will grow faster. Hydrated farmland will turn a darker brown.

For your crops to grow, you'll have to remain in the buildplate for a few minutes.

PLANTED CROPS
To plant something, just use seeds on a farmland block.

CROPS READY TO HARVEST
To harvest a crop, use a spade, sword, or axe. If you just pick up the crop, you'll only get seeds rather than the grown item.

ADVENTURING ISN'T THE ANSWER TO EVERYTHING IN LIFE—TO COLLECT ITEMS TO BUILD WITH, YOU'LL HAVE TO GET BACK TO THE SOIL AND DO A LITTLE HONEST FARMING!

FENCING

This will stop your mobs in their tracks. It is useful if you're growing crops in the same buildplate—any crops that get trampled will be destroyed.

SHEEP

Keeping animal mobs around can be useful—craft some shears, and you can use sheep as a source of wool.

TREE HUGGER

Plant a sapling (obtainable through tappables) on dirt or grass, and wait a few minutes for it to transform into a full-size tree.

Farmable crops include wheat, carrots, melons, and beets.

BUILDPLATES: WATER AND LAVA

When you place a block of water or lava, it will spread across or down from the initial block. It will flow continuously from this block once placed. To remove the flow, use an empty bucket on the initial block you placed.

Liquid cannot flow up, so you can make a channel to contain water.

Place a solid block over an existing flow to stop it, but if you place it on the origin block, you'll lose that source of water or lava for good.

Water and lava can be collected in a bucket, which will be converted into a bucket of water or lava in your inventory (this cannot be used again until you've emptied it).

BUILDING ISN'T JUST ABOUT SOLID BLOCKS—THERE ARE LIQUIDS AVAILABLE TO PLAY WITH, TOO! BUT USE THEM CAREFULLY, SO YOU DON'T DROWN YOUR BUILD . . . OR BURN IT DOWN . . .

Lava will burn wooden and other flammable blocks if it flows into them.

To generate an infinite source of water, dig a 2 x 2 hole, and place two buckets of water diagonally opposite. You can now remove water without drying up the hole.

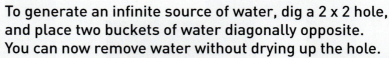

A bucket of lava can be used as a smelting fuel source (see pages 26-27)—it's even more powerful than a coal block. Water will drown mobs, and lava burns them (producing cooked meat from mobs that drop meat). You can also find buckets of mud, which will behave the same as water.

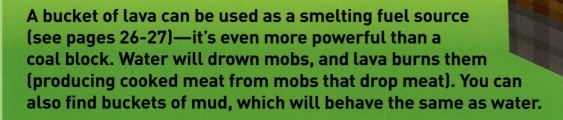

CRAFTING

SICK OF WAITING FOR A BLOCK YOU'RE AFTER TO JUST TURN UP ON YOUR TRAVELS? TIME TO GET CRAFTING.

Select the type of item you'd like to craft, or view everything available in "all items."

Here's where you'll find an item that's currently being crafted or is finished and ready to be picked up.

Sort the item list by name, rarity, or the quantity that you can currently make.

Search for an item by name.

The green border indicates uncommon rarity—different colors indicate different rarities.

Items currently available to craft— the number shows how many you can craft based on the ingredients you have. No number means you can only make one.

Unavailable items require ingredients that you haven't yet collected.

Once you've decided what to craft, tap on the recipe to see more information about the item.

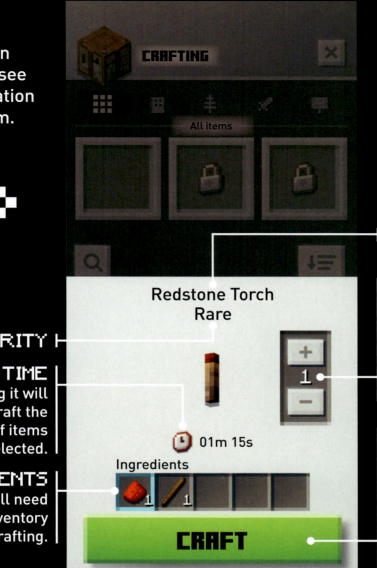

CRAFTING

All items

ITEM NAME

Redstone Torch
Rare

ITEM RARITY

ITEM QUANTITY
How many blocks you want to craft—you can only increase this if you have enough ingredients in your inventory.

TIME
How long it will take to craft the number of items you've selected.

01m 15s

THE CRAFT BUTTON
Tap to begin crafting—if you don't have the right ingredients yet, you'll get an error message.

Ingredients

INGREDIENTS
What you'll need in your inventory to start crafting.

CRAFT

Crafting times include time that passes when you're not playing the game. For a five-minute recipe, you can start crafting, exit the app, then return five minutes later, and your item will be ready for you.

SMELTING

NOT EVERYTHING CAN BE OBTAINED BY CRAFTING—SOMETIMES YOU'LL NEED TO ADD SOME FIRE TO THE EQUATION.

The basic interface works in the same way as crafting, but if you tap on the item you want to smelt, things are a little different . . .

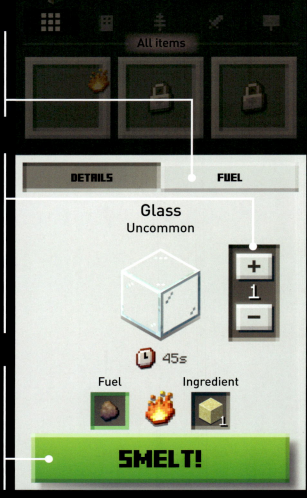

Smelting requires ingredients and fuel. Tap 'fuel' to add or change your fuel source.

You can only increase the number of blocks you want to smelt if you have enough ingredients in your inventory. It may require an adjustment to your fuel.

Once you've selected the ingredients and fuel, hit 'smelt!' to start. If 'insufficient fuel' is displayed, you'll need to adjust your fuel source.

You can only line up a maximum of 64 of an item to be crafted or smelted.

You may need to increase how much fuel you want to use depending on the type of fuel and how many items you want to smelt.

You can select any burnable items in your inventory as fuel—even wooden tools—but coal blocks (which can be crafted from nine pieces of coal) are the best fuel, and they will last longer than other sources.

Smelting is particularly important to turn ore you've mined during adventures into usable material. Smelt iron ore to get iron ingots, which you'll need to craft strong, hard-wearing iron tools.

USEFUL RECIPES

THERE ARE HUNDREDS OF ITEMS TO BE FOUND, MINED, OR CRAFTED IN THE GAME. HERE ARE SOME PARTICULARLY USEFUL BLOCKS AND TOOLS, PLUS WHAT YOU'LL NEED TO CRAFT OR SMELT THEM.

ITEM/BLOCK	WHAT DO YOU NEED?	WHY DO YOU WANT IT?
Sticks	Two planks (from any tree type) will make four sticks.	Can be used to make tools, torches, and other useful items.
Pickaxe	Two sticks and three planks, cobblestone, iron, gold, OR diamond	You need at least an iron pickaxe to mine certain blocks, including gold and redstone.
Sword	Two sticks and two planks, cobblestone, iron, gold, OR diamond	The better the materials you use, the more damage you'll do to enemy mobs.
Torch	One coal and one stick will make four torches.	Essential to light up dark places.
Shears	Two iron ingots	With a pair of shears, you can trim sheep mobs to collect wool.
Dye	Various flowers	You can then dye wool to make blocks and items of different colors.

ITEM/BLOCK	WHAT DO YOU NEED?	WHY DO YOU WANT IT?
Glass	Sand	Transparent blocks that can also be used to craft windows.
Bow	Three sticks and three strings	Can be used to attack enemies from a distance (with arrows).
Arrow	One flint, one stick, and one feather will make four arrows.	Can be used to attack enemies from a distance (with a bow).
Hoe	Two sticks and two planks, cobblestone, iron, gold, OR diamond	Use on dirt to allow you to plant seeds, which will grow into crops.
Spade	Two sticks and one plank, cobblestone, iron, gold, OR diamond	It will help you dig through soil faster.
Axe	Two sticks and three planks, cobblestone, iron, gold, OR diamond	You can chop through wood faster.
Flint and Steel	One flint and one iron ingot	With these you can start fires.
Bucket	Three iron ingots	Use this to transport water and lava between and within buildplates.
String	One cobweb makes nine strings.	Essential for crafting bows and other items.

On the crafting screen, go to the sort button and select 'show all recipes' to see a full list of items and their recipes within the game.

BUILDPLATES: MINECARTS

A minecart placed on a downhill stretch of track will follow the pull of gravity.

The basic rail will form the bulk of your track—this can only be placed on top of blocks.

A piece of rail will automatically curve if placed to connect two other pieces running in different directions, and it will rise or lower to meet a section with a one-block difference in height.

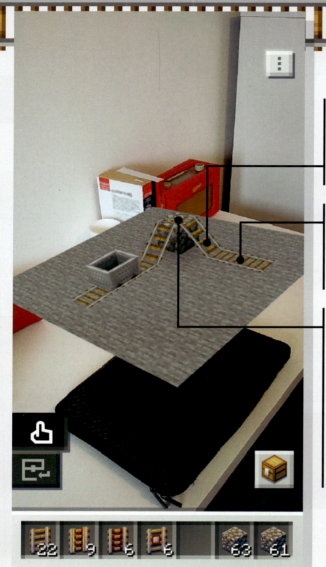

GET MOVING
Push a minecart along a rail by angling your device so you're directly behind it, then move forward to 'hit' it.

Pushing minecarts is easier in play mode—you can just walk 'into' them.

ONE OF THE COOLEST PARTS OF MINECRAFT IS THE ABILITY TO BUILD RIDES AND MECHANISMS USING MINECARTS AND RAILS—AND THEY'RE BOTH AVAILABLE IN MINECRAFT EARTH!

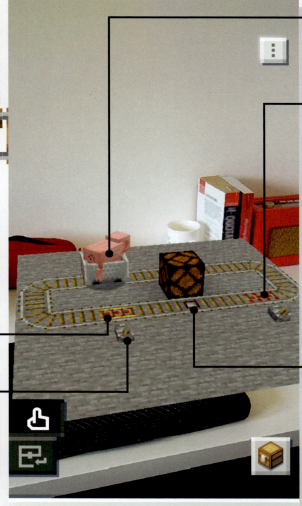

Place a mob on the square next to a minecart, and it will get into the cart.

If powered with redstone, activator rails will act as an ejector seat for any mobs riding the cart. Why not try it out with an unsuspecting test subject?

A section of powered rail will, if connected to redstone power, accelerate a minecart that moves onto it. This only works if the minecart is already in motion.

Detector rails can be used as a type of switch. Place a redstone lamp next to a rail, and a minecart passing over it will turn it on.

The powered and activator rails here are powered using levers, but any redstone power source will work.

BUILDPLATES: REDSTONE

The basics of redstone construction involve something that requires power and something that provides it.

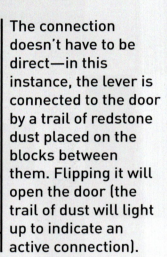

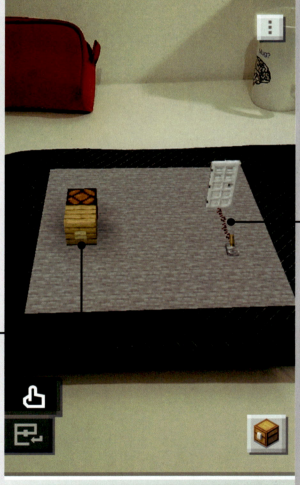

The connection doesn't have to be direct—in this instance, the lever is connected to the door by a trail of redstone dust placed on the blocks between them. Flipping it will open the door (the trail of dust will light up to indicate an active connection).

Pressing the button on the block next to a redstone lamp will temporarily cause it to light up.

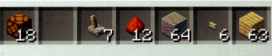

But redstone can do more than provide simple controls. Assemble the pictured blocks in the following configuration:

1 noteblock

2 redstone dust

2 repeaters

2 blocks of planks

1 redstone torch

Once correctly assembled (the directions of the repeaters must match the pictures), you'll have a redstone 'clock' that sends a redstone signal after a regular time period. This works because the repeaters introduce a delay in the transmission of the signal.

HERE ARE SOME OF THE REDSTONE COMPONENTS YOU'LL ENCOUNTER IN THE GAME, WHERE TO FIND AND HOW TO CRAFT THEM, AND WHAT YOU CAN USE THEM FOR . . .

COMPONENT		WHERE / HOW	USE
Redstone ore		Mine these blocks in adventures to obtain one redstone, no smelting required.	N/A
Redstone		One redstone block can be crafted to nine redstone.	Place on top of other blocks to leave trails of dust that connect redstone components together.
Redstone block		Nine redstone	Powers redstone dust and components.
Redstone torch		One redstone, one stick	Powers redstone dust and components.
Redstone lamp		Found in chests	Lights up when activated with a redstone signal.

COMPONENT	WHERE / HOW	USE
Redstone repeater	Three stone, two redstone lamps, one redstone	Can be used to repeat and delay a redstone signal.
Noteblock	One redstone, eight planks (of any wood)	Will play a musical note when activated. You can change the note by tapping the block in interact mode.
Tripwire hook	One iron ingot, one stick, two planks (of any wood) makes two hooks	Place two of these facing each other on the sides of blocks, and attach a string. Any mob or player that tries to pass through the string will activate a redstone signal.
TNT	Found in chests or adventures	With a trail of redstone dust and a means of activation, get ready for something to go BOOM!
Lever	One stick, one cobblestone	Once flipped, will leave a redstone signal active until it's flipped back.
Button	One plank (of any wood)	Will temporarily send a redstone signal.
Pressure plate	Two planks (of any wood) or two stone	If correctly positioned on play mode buildplates, these will activate when you're physically standing on top of them!

ADVENTURES

GOT YOUR HEAD AROUND THE BASICS? MAYBE IT'S TIME TO HEAD OUT IN SEARCH OF A MINECRAFT EARTH ADVENTURE!

If you're having trouble locating adventures, try areas like parks or public squares, since they're designed to spawn in open spaces. You'll need to be fairly close to the adventure to activate it—just being within your proximity ring isn't quite close enough.

Choose the items you take carefully, since you won't be able to access your full inventory without leaving the adventure and starting again.

If you find an adventure with gray blocks in a yellow hexagon, you're the first person to try it!

There are four different types of adventure to try out in Minecraft Earth . . .

Peaceful: Not the most exciting, but you can practice your mining skills without being attacked.

Hostile: Weapons set to go, battle through an entire horde of hostile mobs to uncover extra loot.

Puzzle: These adventures contain a puzzle to be solved by moving or activating blocks.

Mystery: Be ready for anything because you can't be sure what to expect!

PLACE

When placing the adventure try to pick a spot you can access from all sides.

Always make sure to have a thorough dig down into the adventure plate—the more valuable blocks like iron and gold ore are often buried near the bottom.

As your tools wear out with use, save your good ones (e.g. iron pickaxes) for the blocks that require them (e.g. gold, diamond).

If you're having trouble reaching certain parts of the adventure, try holding your device higher or at a different angle, or try moving to a different position.

TAKE NOTE OF WHAT YOU MIGHT FACE, AND MAKE THE MOST OF THE OPPORTUNITIES THE ADVENTURES OFFER!

Killing mobs will reward you with items and experience. Equip a sword or other weapon to do this most effectively.

As a last resort, you can always try the old 'get rid of the mobs by dropping a bucket of water or lava' trick! Although you won't get any experience points for killing them this way.

Some mobs, such as skeletons, can attack you from a distance once you're within their line of sight, so be ready to retreat—as long as you have space to move into in the real world!

When mobs aren't currently visible, you'll see symbols on screen indicating where they are in relation to you. They might not be on the same plane, though—you might have to dig down into the buildplate to find them.

If you run out of health, you'll automatically be taken back to the map, and you will lose anything you collected AND everything in your hotbar.

If you're worried that you're about to die, try to manually exit the adventure and return to the map. It's not a dignified retreat, but at least you won't lose the items you've taken with you.

Adventures have time limits—this symbol will appear to let you know you're almost out of time. When your time is up, you'll automatically be dropped back to the map.

Mobs can leave the adventure plate if they reach or are on ground level, so watch out—even the real world isn't safe!

Think carefully before you start collecting blocks and items in puzzle adventures—they might be needed where they are to solve the puzzle, which will unlock more valuable blocks than those you can collect at the start.

MOBS

AN INEVITABLE PART OF AN ADVENTURER'S LIFESTYLE ARE THE HOSTILE MOBS THAT STAND BETWEEN YOU AND ALL THAT LOVELY LOOT. SO BEFORE YOU ENTER AN ADVENTURE, HERE ARE SOME VITAL STATS AND INFO TO KNOW ABOUT THEM!

MOB	ATTITUDE	DETAILS	DAMAGE / HEALTH	DROPS
Zombie	Hostile	This is the classic Minecraft mob—not too much to worry about on their own, but slightly harder to kill if found in great numbers.	Three damage/ twenty health	Rotten flesh, iron ingot (rarely)
Spider	Hostile	Even if you avoid their bites, you may find that their cobwebs block your way—use a sword to cut through them.	Three damage/ sixteen health	String

MOB	ATTITUDE	DETAILS	DAMAGE / HEALTH	DROPS
Skeleton	Hostile	One of the game's more lethal mobs—you need to take them out quickly, because if you can see them, they can fire arrows at you. Get ready to duck!	Fires arrows. Twenty health	Arrows, bones
Creeper	Hostile	These nasty critters have an alarming tendency to explode when they get too close to you.	Explodes when close to player. Twenty health	Gunpowder

On the crafting screen, go to the sort button and select "show all recipes" to see a full list of items and their recipes within the game. See what you can make with the loot that mobs drop.

MOB	ATTITUDE	DETAILS	HEALTH	DROPS
Chicken	Neutral	If you place these mobs on buildplates, they'll occasionally lay eggs.	Four	Feather, chicken (food)
Cow	Neutral	Use a bucket on this mob to get milk.	Ten	Leather, beef
Sheep	Neutral	Use shears on this mob to get wool without killing it.	Eight	White wool, mutton
Pig	Neutral	Sometimes found as muddy pigs, from which you can get mud using a bucket.	Ten	Pork chop
Rabbit	Neutral	Also available in larger but functionally identical jumbo format.	Three	Rabbit hide, rabbit (food), rabbit foot (rarely)
Mob of Me	Neutral	It's you . . . but not you? You'll find one of these in the buildplate you're given at level five.	Twenty	Mob of Me

MOB	ATTITUDE	DETAILS	HEALTH	DROPS
Parrot	Neutral	This mob can copy the sounds made by any other nearby mob, so could moo like a cow or mimic something hostile!	Six	Feather
Polar bear	Neutral	An ice-cold mob, it can be found in the level twenty buildplate.	Thirty	Salmon, fish
Cluckshroom	Neutral	After tapping on a chicken, you may discover that it has become one of these peculiar creatures. This bird leaves trails of mushrooms behind when placed on a buildplate!	Four	Feather, chicken (food)
Moobloom	Neutral	Tappable cows occasionally turn out to be this curious, cowlike creature, which leaves trails of buttercups.	Ten	Leather, beef

You can also access even rarer mobs that are only made available for limited time periods or during special events.

CHALLENGING BEHAVIOR

CHALLENGES ALLOW YOU TO EARN REWARDS AS YOU PLAY THE GAME. ACCESS THEM THROUGH THE MAP SCREEN.

There are four types of challenges:

Daily must be completed within twenty-four hours.

Weekly must be completed within a week (Monday to Sunday).

Career can be completed at any time.

Event is only available at special events.

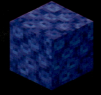

Once a challenge is completed, you need to enter the challenges screen and hit collect to access your rewards.

For completing a challenge, you can earn:

➕ Experience points: Earn enough of these and you'll reach the next level.

➕ Rubies: These can be used to unlock new buildplates and speed up crafting.

SETTINGS ✕

Music   100%

Sound Effects   100%

Vibration   **ON**

Precision Mode   **OFF**

Bright Mode   **OFF**

Language

ENGLISH (UK)   >

minecrafter1485   **SIGN OUT**

Safety Video   **WATCH**

                            VIEW

Find a bug?   **REPORT**

In this mode, the screens for buildplate and adventure are given a crosshair target, making it easier to be more precise in how you aim—only blocks under the crosshair will be affected by your actions.

In this mode, the brightness of blocks is increased—this can make it easier to see blocks of different types, especially when digging down into dark spaces.

This will log you out of your account—useful if you're sharing your device with someone else.

You can also access these settings while in buildplates or adventures by tapping the [. . .] box in the top right corner.

FRIENDS AND EVENTS

WANT SOME COMPANY? NO WORRIES, MINECRAFT EARTH HAS SEVERAL MULTIPLAYER FEATURES BUILT IN—HERE'S HOW TO ACCESS THEM.

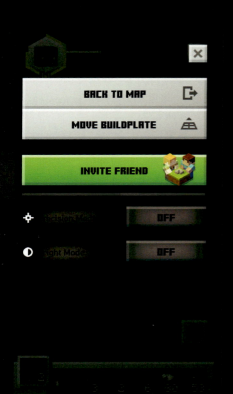

INVITE FRIEND

Friends can scan this screen from the "Join Friend" button.

To let someone else visit one of your buildplates, open it in either build or play modes, and tap the [. . .] button.

From this menu, tap 'Invite friend' to generate a sharing screen.

BEWARE!

Only share your buildplates in build mode with someone you trust—any changes they make will be permanent. In play mode, all changes will be reverted once you exit the buildplate.

At certain times and in certain locations, there are Minecraft Earth events at which a code will be available. Scanning it allows you to access an adventure only available at that specific location.

The person you want to share with needs to open up this menu item and select 'Join friend,' which will open their camera. Once the code is scanned, they'll be able to enter the buildplate you shared with them.

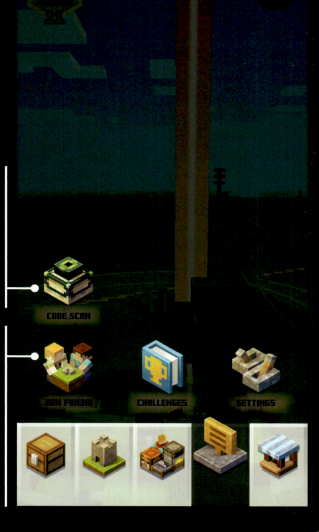

CODE SCAN

JOIN FRIEND   CHALLENGES   SETTINGS

You have to be in the same physical location as the person (or people) you want to share your build with in order for this to work. No one can access a buildplate that you aren't already playing yourself, and if you leave the buildplate anyone else exploring it will be disconnected.

BUILD IDEA: TOWERS AND MONUMENTS

Sick of waiting for someone to build you a monument? Why not build one for yourself—or rather, your Minecraft character?

To commemorate your Minecrafting abilities, why not show the statue holding a block up high? Build the arm sticking out in front of your character. Add two blocks at the end, then remove the first, leaving the second floating in midair.

To give the effect of a statue, we've used gray blocks of andesite for the face and arms.

Cobblestone makes a good basic building material—here we've used it to make a square base. See pages 52–53 for a way to collect lots of it, if you find yourself running out.

Wool is a great way to add detail to your builds since it's available in many different colors.

MINECRAFT EARTH'S AR COMPONENTS MEAN THAT YOU CAN CREATE EPIC BUILDS AT HOME, THEN IN PLAY MODE SEE WHAT THEY LOOK AT FULL SIZE OUT IN THE WORLD. HERE ARE COUPLE OF IDEAS TO GET YOU STARTED . . .

Test the game's limits with a tower. For this simple but effective build, start with a flat plate.

In the center, place a 2 x 2 square of cobblestone (any stackable block will work for this). Then just repeat, repeat, and repeat.

Getting bored with just going up? Add some detail, like this viewing platform, to help pigs get a sense of perspective!

STAND BACK!
You might want to get some distance from this build to fully appreciate it!

The maximum height of a buildplate is 221 blocks—can you get your tower blocks that high? You might need to place your buildplate on the floor and stand over it to be able to get at it from the right angle.

BUILD IDEA: UP ON THE FARM

Place a cobblestone block in each corner.

Remove all the blocks on the buildplate, then create a cobblestone floor one block below ground level.

Stack cobblestone on the corner blocks until each column is eleven blocks high, then connect the first, fourth, seventh, and tenth blocks of each column to form a frame for your farm.

WANT TO GET INTO FARMING, BUT ALWAYS FINDING YOURSELF RUNNING OUT OF BUILDPLATES? THIS ULTRAEFFICIENT VERTICAL FARM GIVES YOU ALL THE SPACE YOU NEED IN A SINGLE BUILDPLATE.

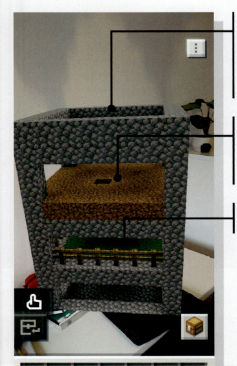

Fill the square in the top with cobblestone, then add a cobblestone wall around the edge. Leave a one-block hole near the center of the level.

Fill the square in the middle with dirt blocks. Build it up one more level, and leave a one-block hole below the hole in the cobblestone layer above.

Fill with grass blocks. Place fence around the cobblestone edges.

Empty water buckets here to create water storage space—it will also flow down to the next level.

Here you'll create a farm by using a hoe on the soil and planting seeds.

Here's an ideal pen for sheep, so you can stock up on wool anytime you need it.

And safely tucked away below it, here's your lava storage unit.

BUILD IDEA: STONE FACTORY

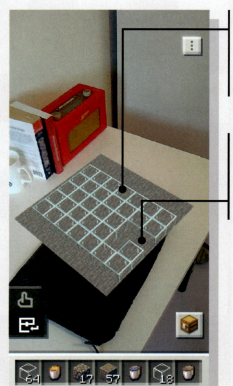

Start with a one-block-high base, five blocks by seven blocks across. We've used glass, but any nonflammable material will do.

Leave a gap at the front in the shape and position shown—this will be where you'll collect the blocks from.

Build up the last row until it's three blocks high. Do the same with the row in front of it, but leave gaps—this is where you'll add the ingredients.

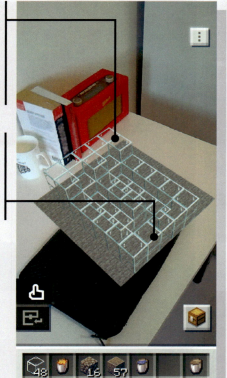

Build two channels in front of the gaps you left by building up the blocks around the edge and in the center.

If you like, you can put another row of blocks on top to seal off the channels and make it look tidier—just make sure the two spaces at the back are left open.

GOT A BIG CONSTRUCTION PROJECT IN MIND, BUT CAN'T FACE GOING OUT TO COLLECT MORE STONE FOR IT? THIS BUILD WILL PROVIDE YOU WITH A LIMITLESS SUPPLY.

First, place a lava source block—using the bucket—in the first slot (on the left).

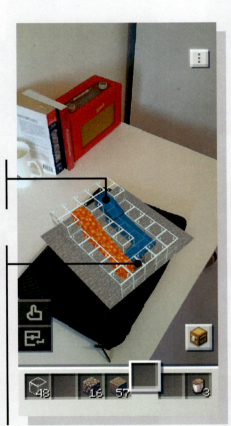

Now place a water source block in the second slot.

The water and lava will flow along the channel you've left—where they meet, a cobblestone block will be created. Collect the block, and another will appear in its place—continue until you've got enough cobblestone.

If you use a bucket of mud instead of a bucket of water, the factory will produce blocks of dirt instead.

BUILD IDEA: REDSTONE FUN

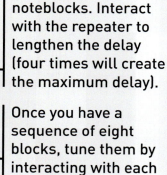

Place a button on a block to act as a trigger.

Place a sequence of repeaters followed by noteblocks. Interact with the repeater to lengthen the delay (four times will create the maximum delay).

Once you have a sequence of eight blocks, tune them by interacting with each as follows:

Block 1—10 times
Block 2—10 times
Block 3—11 times
Block 4—13 times
Block 5—13 times
Block 6—11 times
Block 7—10 times
Block 8—8 times

Press the button and you should hear the start to Beethoven's *Ode to Joy!*

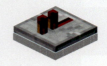

REDSTONE CAN BE USED TO CONSTRUCT ALL KINDS OF WEIRD AND WONDERFUL DEVICES. WITH NOTEBLOCKS AND REDSTONE LAMPS, YOU CAN EVEN CREATE SOUND AND LIGHT SEQUENCES.

You can increase the delay between different parts of the sequence by chaining repeaters, but make sure they're facing in the same direction.

You can also create sequences of multiple blocks—here the button and the repeaters each connect to two redstone lamps.

Redstone dust must connect to the block you want it to power—if the trail isn't going into the block, you may need to try a different arrangement.

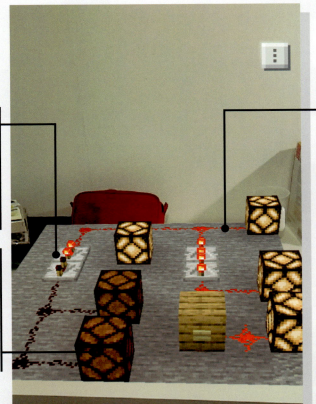

You could even try combining noteblocks as well as redstone lamps into the same sequence, triggering sound and light at the same points.

BUILD IDEA: THE GREAT MINECRAFT RACE

Start by flattening your build—here we've used a grass surface, but anything you can place rails on will work.

Starting from a corner, lay out a course of rails running into the center. Mark the end with a cobblestone block, but leave an empty space between the last rail and the cobblestone.

You'll need access to at least a 16 x 16-sized buildplate for this.

Repeat the course from the image above on the opposite side.

Add detector rails to the gaps you left at the end, and place noteblocks and redstone lamps next to them.

Place minecarts on the rails in each corner. Mobs are optional but funnier.

You can always make more complex tracks (with up or downhill sections), but if you want to make them fair, both halves should be a mirror image of each other.

SHOWING OFF YOUR AMAZING BUILDS TO YOUR FRIENDS IS ALL VERY WELL, BUT HERE'S ONE YOU CAN ACTUALLY INVITE THEM INTO FOR SOME PROPER AR MULTIPLAYER ACTION.

Now, enter into play mode, invite a friend into your build, and line up behind your minecarts. On your mark, get set, go! When the minecarts hit the last rail, the noteblock will sound, the lamp will light, and you'll know who's won.

To be really fair, you could build something that sounds a note on a timer to tell you when to start. See pages 54–55 for some ideas on how to use redstone to do this.

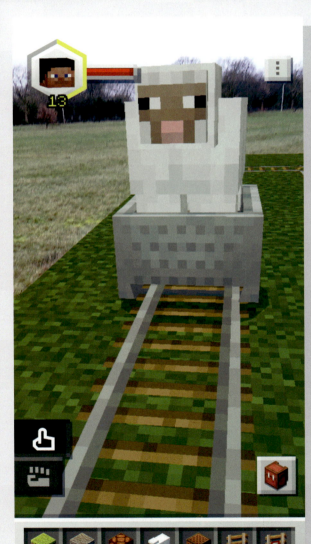

BUILD IDEA: MUSICAL INSTRUMENT

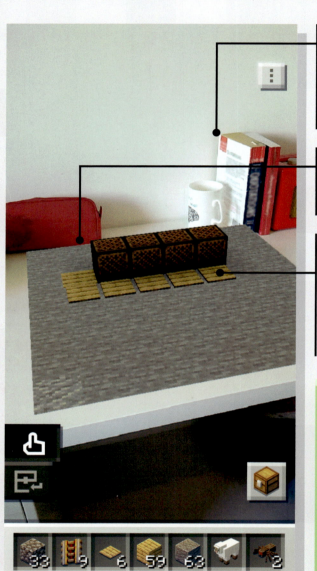

Place the noteblocks, then tune your blocks in interact mode—to make the notes sequential, leave the first block alone, tap the second once, the third twice, etc.

Make the base for your instrument by placing a row of planks (or other wooden blocks) in the ground.

For the keys of your instrument, place a row of pressure plates in front of the noteblocks. Moving over each pressure plate will cause the noteblock in front of it to sound.

The block beneath a noteblock affects how it sounds:

Dirt block—harp
Wooden block—bass
Sand block—snare
Gold block—bell
Wool block—guitar

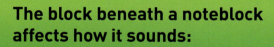

EVER WANT A GIANT MUSICAL INSTRUMENT THAT YOU CAN CONTROL WITH YOUR FEET? MINECRAFT EARTH HAS YOU COVERED, SO GET BUILDING, THEN GET READY TO SHOW OFF YOUR MUSICAL SKILLS!

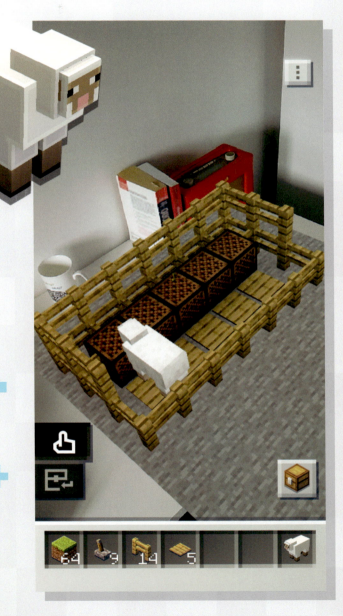

To get the full effect, head outside and enter your buildplate in play mode. You can now walk back and forth across your build to play your life-size instrument!

If you're struggling to hear your creation, you may need to adjust the volume of the music in the settings menu.

You're not the only one who can trigger a pressure plate: Place some fences around your instrument and add a sheep to experience some improvised mob jazz!

BUILD IDEA: THE GAUNTLET

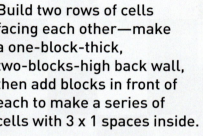

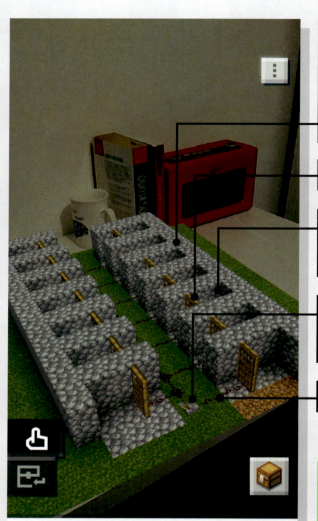

Build two rows of cells facing each other—make a one-block-thick, two-blocks-high back wall, then add blocks in front of each to make a series of cells with 3 x 1 spaces inside.

Block off the back two blocks of each cell with a door.

Looking down into the cells from above, drop mobs into each cell—the more dangerous, the better!

Place a lever at the end of the trail. When you interact with it, it should open or close all the doors.

Run a trail of redstone dust connecting all the doors.

Hostile mobs that you can store in your inventory and place in your builds are available through tappables—skeletons in stone, spiders in trees, and creepers from grass. They're rare, so it may take a while to build up a good collection.

THIS BUILD WILL ALLOW YOU TO CONSTRUCT THE ULTIMATE DEATH TRAP TO TRY OUT YOUR COMBAT SKILLS OR CHALLENGE YOUR FRIENDS.

Now, load your build in play mode, equip your best sword, and pull the lever to see if you can survive a trip through The Gauntlet. Here we've tested it with some highly trained chickens!

On bigger plates, you could build a more complex version of this build—why not try constructing an entire labyrinth full of nasty mobs?

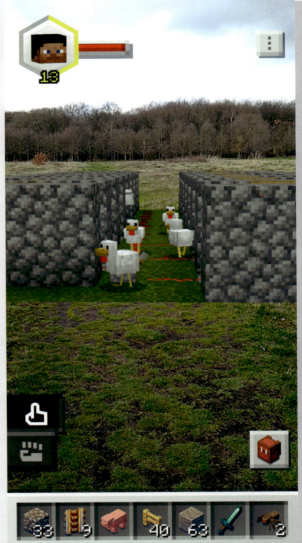

BUILD IDEA: TNT TRAP HOUSE

Prepare your buildplate by digging down and building an underground pit at least five to six blocks deep.

Fill it with lava. This will finish off anyone that somehow survives the TNT! You'll need three or four buckets to fill a 6 x 6 pit like this.

If TNT is placed over an empty block, it will start falling when triggered, so might not blow up what you expect.

Seal up your pit with a layer of grass to hide it away.

Now lay your trap: Start building a house with one block raised above the ground.

Give your house an iron door with a lever on a block next to it—hopefully, your victim will assume that the lever will only open the door.

Lay redstone behind the lever block, and then place some TNT blocks behind it, into the floor of the house.